HOW TO CREATE YOUR WEBSITE

For Writers and Other Clueless Souls

Also by Mateja Klaric

Self-Publishing Made Easy series

Book 1
How to Self-Publish Your Book:
The Fast, Free & Easy Way

Book 2
You Self-Published, Now What?
How to Promote Your Book

Book 3
How to Create Your Website:
For Writers and Other Clueless Souls

The Fox & White Rabbit

The Story of the Fox and White Rabbit
(not your ordinary fable)

HOW TO CREATE YOUR WEBSITE

For Writers and Other Clueless Souls

Mateja Klaric

How to Create Your Website:
For Writers and Other Clueless Souls

First edition, April 22, 2019, published by Mateja Klaric
Third book in the series Self-Publishing Made Easy
ISDN: 9781096386803

Author: Mateja Klaric
Proofreading: James Reeves
Cover & book design: Mateja Klaric
Cover photo: Icons8 (icons8.com)
matejaklaric.com

Dedicated to all those who have stood by my side in the time of need. Thank you for your invaluable help.

Thank you, Daniel Sinnathamby,
for your kindness and support.

And special thanks to you, James Reeves.
None of my books would have been written and published without your sincere friendship and generosity.

.

TABLE OF CONTENTS

WHO IS THIS BOOK FOR?

Almost everyone today, and even more so writers and bloggers, are faced with the need for a website or blog. In the case of a writer, that would be a place where you can showcase your books, build your email list, and make it easy for those interested in your work to contact you.

If you want to have a professional online presence, you'll have to buy your custom domain and create a related email address. For this, you'll need a hosting service and a website builder or a platform where you can build and host your website. There are many different options, and it's easy to feel overwhelmed and confused by that alone.

But that's far from the only challenge. Nowadays, cyber security threats are everywhere, and you simply cannot avoid having to deal with them. If you neglect that, search engines might warn or prevent users from visiting your website, your domain could get stolen, your subscribers' data abused, and your website hacked.

If you find all this a bit much to handle, then this book is for you. It will lead you by the hand through every step of the process – from buying a domain to creating a secure, professional, user-friendly, and successful website. You'll find many useful apps and tools in this book too. They will help keeping your website healthy and optimized.

All this is written in an easy-to-follow and simple manner. Technical terms are explained so that you can understand what they mean and why they are important. This book takes the scary and overwhelming part of website building and hosting away. It will make everything so much easier for you.

WHO AM I TO WRITE IT?

I used to be clueless and utterly confused by all the online advice regarding websites. I've seen more than one writer recommending WordPress, accompanied by a claim how you can have your website up and running there in no more than a few hours.

In my experience, nothing could be further from the truth. What's more, I would say that this is the most insidious advice I have ever received. Would you buy a plot and build your house there in but a few hours? Well, don't think you can create a decent website that fast either.

As a clueless soul, I trusted this horrible advice only to end up wasting a whole lot of time and money while already being short on both. I had no idea what I was doing; I kept buying services I didn't need, making costly mistakes, and overpaying for just about everything.

After over two years of testing and learning it all the hard way, I finally mastered everything one needs to know to create a functional, cost-efficient, and secure website without losing one's mind in the process. I'm now sharing all this with you so that you don't have to repeat the mistakes that I made.

NOTE:
There are no affiliate links in this book. Recommendations are based entirely on my sincere satisfaction with these apps, tools and services.

1. THE BASICS

Think of your website as your online home. Much like your physical home, a website comes with an address, a plot, a building or a structure, and a mailbox. Similar terminology applies in both cases and referring to a domain as a property is a common terminology used by Google.

When it comes to your virtual home, your domain name represents your online address, a website builder or hosting service gives you an online plot where you can create and maintain your online home (website), and an email address plays the role of your online mailbox.

Like with your home, there are quite a few things you need to take care of to make your website functional, secure, and affordable. That's why it's important to know where to begin, in what order to proceed, and how everything works.

If you have the time, it might be a good idea to take the free *Internet 101* course at Khan Academy [1]. While not necessary for building a website, this interesting introductory course will give you an insight into how the internet works and explain the fundamental issues, such as security.

Let's start with a to-do list of everything you'll need to take care of to build and maintain your website. In the following chapters, you'll become closely familiar with each of the items on this list.

To-do list

This a basic list of things you'll need to do. Following the order in which these activities are listed here will make the process faster, easier, and cost-efficient.

1. **Choose a hosting service and buy a domain**
2. **Create your email address**
3. **Create a temporary landing page**
4. **Redirect your domain to the landing page**
5. **Clarify your website goals**
6. **Choose your website platform**
7. **Design and build your website**
8. **Take care of SEO**
9. **Connect your domain and launch**

Don't worry, I'll guide you through all of this. Two things you'll need to do for a start are buying your domain and choosing a hosting plan. You need hosting so that you can manage your domain and emails. But what exactly is a domain and how does this work? That's the topic of the next chapter.

2. INTRODUCTION TO DOMAINS

The main role of the domain name is to serve as your online address. In the case of my website, that's matejaklaric.com. This makes it possible for people to easily find a website in their browser. Ideally, your website's URL will appear high in the search results when people google your name.

Buying a domain will also make it possible for you to create custom email addresses (e.g. you@yourdomain.com). Before we get there, though, there are a few things you need to know about domains. They come in many different forms and that alone can have a positive or negative effect on your website's ranking on Google and other search engines.

Parts of a domain

The main part of a domain is the name you pick for your domain (in my case, matejaklaric) and the extension you choose among many available (e.g. .com, .info…). You might have noticed that the domain name may or may not also include www at the beginning. We'll talk about that too.

Finally, there is a part you see before the domain name in the browser's URL bar as either http:// or https://. All these elements form the website's URL and that's what makes it possible for Google and other browsers to find and display a website, for instance: https://www.matejaklaric.com.

All these parts play various important roles, and it's thus crucial that you understand them. They matter for more than one reason and can affect a website's security, functionality, ranking in search results, your privacy, as well as the cost of running your website.

Domain name and extension

Domain name is the easy part – when buying your domain, simply put in the name you would like to register as your domain name (e.g. your real or pen name) and select the desired extension (e.g. .com). For a writer, it's best to use the name you publish under and the common extension .com.

There are plenty of other extensions available too, such as .info, .org, and .blog. Established companies and brands often buy their domain name with all of the most common extensions to prevent abuse of their brand. That, however, can get quite expensive and if you are an unknown writer, you don't have to worry about that just yet.

If you nevertheless want to secure different extensions for your domain name, be aware that you'll have to pay a yearly fee for each of them. Since you cannot buy a domain name once and for all, you'll have to keep renewing it. You will also have to manage each of these domains separately, for the same domain name with a different extension is treated as a separate domain.

Geo extensions, such as .eu (European Union) or .ca (Canada) are usually cheaper but unless you plan on only writing for the local market, using such extensions could backfire when it comes to Google search results. If you use local geo extension, Google might rank your site higher locally but lower globally [2].

Another, even more important issue is privacy. Unlike with generic top-level domains (e.g. .com), you won't be able to protect your private information if you opt for geo extension. This means that everyone will be able to get access to your private information, such as your email. You'll find more on that in Chapter 3 *Privacy & Security*.

Email address

Once you buy a domain and hosting plan, you'll be able to use your domain to create a custom email address. You can put whatever you want in front of the @yourdomain.com, for instance, something like info@yourdomain.com.

You'll need a hosting service with a plan that comes with email and not just domain hosting for that, though. Be aware that not every hosting service offers this option. You'll find all you need to know about this in Chapter 4 *Hosting Services* and Chapter 5 *Managing Domains & Emails*.

Subdomains

Subdomain is created when you add a prefix to your domain. As an example, members.matejaklaric.com is a subdomain I use for a website where I publish content for members. It's quite easy to create a subdomain at your hosting service, and you'll learn how to do that in Chapter 5 *Managing Domains & Emails*.

Using subdomains became popular because it's free and thus a cost-efficient way of publishing several websites on different subdomains while only paying a renewal fee for the main domain name. For this, however, you'll need a domain hosting plan that lets you create subdomains (you'll find more on that in Chapter 4 *Hosting Services*).

In the case of my subdomain, for instance, I only pay the yearly fee for my main domain name matejaklaric.com. I can then create subdomains for free and use them as custom domains for different websites. For instance, I use my main domain and its subdomain to host two different websites: www.matejaklaric.com and members.matejaklaric.com.

You might have noticed the www in front of my main domain name – that too is a form of a subdomain, and the domain without www is called naked domain.

Naked domain vs. www

A special and commonly used form of a subdomain starts with www. Originally, all URLs started with www. It lately, however, became trendy to use a naked domain as a preferred domain instead.

While naked domains indeed look nicer and simpler, there is an ongoing debate on whether that's recommended. Some experts point out that using a naked domain without www can cause various technical and safety issues, especially when your site starts to get more traffic [3].

When you buy a domain name, you get a naked domain, and you'll have to make a decision regarding your www or no-www preference later. This, however, will to a large degree also depend on the website builder or platform you choose.

SSL and http:// vs. https://

If you pay attention to the content in the browser's URL bar, you've probably noticed that in some cases browsers display a red security warning next to some URLs or even prevent you from visiting some websites.

That's because these websites aren't secured with an SSL certificate and thus represent a security threat. This is what the difference between http:// and https:// protocols is all about. If your website is only delivered through the http:// protocol, this means that it is not secure. Any information sent through such websites could thus be intercepted, altered, and abused by unsavory characters [4].

Google and other browsers warn the users about this and punish these websites by lowering their rank in the browser's search results. To avoid such issues and make sure your website is displayed through https:// protocol, make sure your website hosting comes with an SSL certificate. You'll find more on this in Chapter 7 *Website Builders & Blogs*.

Domain privacy and security issues

Another thing you need to be careful about are privacy and security issues that come with owning a domain. Unless you take steps to prevent that, your private information, such as your name and email address will become publicly available as soon as you become the domain's registered owner.

This will open the door to spam and abuse. Just like any other property, your domain name can be stolen, and that's another thing you need to protect yourself from. You will find the recommended steps in Chapter 3 *Privacy & Security*. It's one of the most important chapters in the book.

Where to buy a domain

There are three main types of companies that sell domain names, but not all these options are equal or can be recommended:

- Registrars
- Hosting services
- Website builders

Of the three options, using the latter as a domain and email hosting service is not recommended. The main reason for this is that you need full control over your domain regardless of the website builder or platform you use. That's important in case you want to switch to another platform later.

If you use a separate hosting service for domain and email hosting, it will be very easy to switch to another website builder with little downtime and no email or domain-related issues. This then leaves you with the first two options – registrar or hosting service.

Even if you wanted to buy a domain directly from a registrar, though, most of them only work with resellers (hosting services) or sell only domains without hosting. The best and simplest option for a beginner would thus be to buy a domain at a good hosting service. There are, however, major differences between these as well.

Choosing the right hosting service for your needs will take some time and shouldn't be taken lightly. You'll find all about that in Chapter 4 *Hosting Services*.

The cost of a domain

The cost depends on whether you buy a new or a so-called aged domain. A new domain means that the domain name has not yet been registered by somebody else. Aged domain, on the other hand, has already been registered and the owner might or might not be willing to sell it.

New domains with .com extension usually cost between $10 to $20 per year, depending on your hosting service. The price for aged domains, however, can go into millions. There is a market where people speculate by buying domain names and then try to resell them for as much as they can.

Chances are you'll be able to buy a new domain name if you plan on using your own or pen name and are not famous yet. One of the first things you should do is to secure your name in the form of a domain to avoid having to buy it from a trader later. If you become well-known, not having your domain name registered can come at a high price. Tesla.com, for instance, was sold for $11 MIO [5].

3. PRIVACY & SECURITY

Privacy and security are of paramount importance not only for your website's success but also for your own privacy as well as the safety of your domain. All your hard work can be lost in a blink of an eye if you fail to take precautions, so follow the suggestions you'll find in this chapter.

If you don't, Google and other search engines will punish you. As mentioned before, things such as not having an SSL certificate might even prevent visitors from accessing your website. But that's just the beginning. You need to protect your emails and online property too.

As your website becomes more popular, its value will begin to increase. While this is great, it might also attract the attention of spammers and hackers who have anything but your best interest in mind.

Even if you think no one would care to attack your website or email account, this might not be so. Hackers do this for all sorts of reasons, including for fun or to prove themselves. You'll be even more vulnerable if you use open source platforms and plugins [6].

✓ To-do list

Here is a to-do list of the things you need to pay attention to. Taking care of these things will improve your website's security, protect your privacy, and protect the rights and privacy of your visitors too:

1. Use SSL certificate
2. Create strong passwords
3. Protect your identity and emails

4. Protect your domain with Domain Transfer Lock
5. Beware open source platforms and plugins
6. Guard access to your computer and accounts
7. Know the risk of using Wi-Fi
8. Use reCAPTCHA
9. Use GDPR

Let's take a closer look at the items on this list.

SSL certificate (website and mail client)

SSL certificates are not only used to display your website through a safe https:// protocol, but also to protect your email account and emails [7]. That why you need to take care of both, and you'll have to do this in two separate ways:

- **Website hosting** – install SSL certificate
- **Mail client** – set your account up using SSL option

Most website builders and blogging platforms already come with SSL certificate, but this will also depend on the plan you use. Make sure that your platform and plan include it.

As for emails, your domain hosting service will provide guidelines on how to set up your email account to securely send and receive emails using SSL. You'll find step-by-step instruction on how to do this in Chapter 5 *Managing Domain & Emails.*

Passwords

Among the most common cyber attacks are brute force and dictionary attacks. This means that the hacker somehow finds out or guesses which email address you use for logins and cracks your password using programs specifically developed for the purpose [8].

Ransomware attacks are also increasingly common and costly. In this case, hackers hijack your website or computer and then demand a ransom to unlock it. You can do a lot to prevent such attacks just by using long, complicated, and nonsensical passwords that are hard to crack [9].

Create strong passwords for everything on this list:

- Hosting service login
- Email address password at your hosting service
- Email account login
- Website builder or blog login
- Social media logins
- Your computer login
- Your home Wi-Fi login

Regularly change these passwords and don't use the same ones for more than one account. This will prevent the domino effect in case that a hacker manages to break one of them.

It's not recommended to save important passwords in your browser (especially not passwords related to finances or anything else of value). Also, use two-factor authentication whenever possible.

Identity and email protection

As soon as you buy a domain, your information automatically becomes a part of a database of domain owners and is made public. If you, for instance, buy one of the generic top-level domains (e.g. .com, .org, .net…), ICANN WHOIS database of domain owners will publish this [10].

To prevent your private data from being published, you'll have to use a domain privacy protection option at your hosting service. Usually, hosting companies list this as WHOIS Privacy Protection. This, however, is not possible for geo extensions so choose an extension that can be protected.

To check whether the privacy protection feature has been turned on, visit https://whois.icann.org/en/lookup, insert your domain name in the search window, and click "Lookup." This will open EPP status code information for your domain [11]. If everything is in order, your information should be hidden (status "Not Disclosed").

Use contact forms instead of your email address

Never publish or disclose your email address anywhere online. Hackers and spammers use online crawlers to harvest email addresses from the internet only to abuse them. Try not to make that easy for them [12].

In addition to strong passwords, protect your personal information by hiding your email address and use a contact form on your website instead. Most website builders and many WordPress and Tumblr themes have this option among their basic features.

Domain Transfer Lock

Your domain is vulnerable and can be stolen unless your domain hosting service locks it. Unlocked domains are at risk, so you need to make sure that safety features, such as Domain Transfer Lock, are not only available but also used at your hosting service.

To check whether your domain is locked, use the same procedure you used on ICANN WHOIS website to check for your domain's privacy protection. Just like you did when you checked for that, go to https://whois.icann.org/en/lookup and use the "Lookup" option. If your domain is safely locked, its status should be "clienttransferprohibited."

If you see "OK" instead of "clienttransferprohibited," though, this means that the domain is not locked and can be transferred. Unless you are the one who ordered a transfer, you should contact your hosting company and ask them to lock your domain asap.

Some suggest that your domain is only truly safe if you also lock three other statuses (Server delete, Server update, Server transfer), but some domain hosting services might not be willing or able to do this [13].

Beware open source platforms and tools

WordPress.org is the most popular website platform in the world but also by far the most vulnerable and likely to be targeted by hackers [14]. Other open source platforms, such as Joomla, Drupal, and Magento are also on the list of the platforms with the most hacked websites.

Among the most common reasons for this are software, themes, and plugins that have not been updated regularly or are no longer supported by the developers, which means that they no longer get new security updates. Most security problems with WordPress are due to the use of such plugins.

With open source platforms such as WordPress.org, you'll have to constantly watch for new updates. This includes the updates of your theme and each plugin you use. You'll also have to use a good website hosting service and regularly download backups of your website to your computer [15].

Plugins, themes, and addons

Literally thousands of plugins, themes, and addons have been developed for WordPress alone. While these can make your site look nicer and enhance its functionality, they also present a major security risk.

The reason for this is that anyone can develop, sell, or offer these for free, and since the platforms such as WordPress.org are open source platforms, there are no safety standards in place when it comes to external tools.

Never use themes or plugins unless a developer has a good reputation, high-quality customer support, and has been a well-known member of the WordPress community. Be careful with free plugins too since these may come at a high cost to your website's security [16].

Guard access to your computer and accounts

I once made a mistake of downloading an open source platform Joomla CMS to my computer. The result of this was the ugliest free website I've ever seen, and an annoying error script that constantly kept popping up on my screen.

It took me a while to get rid of that. Since Joomla is an open source platform, there is no customer support service and the only option you have is to post an issue on their forum. Only one developer from India responded to my pleas. He offered help, but asked for a payment and, what's worse, wanted to get access to my computer.

I would have never given an unknown developer access to my computer, and neither should you. Would you just open the door of your home to a "handyman" you've never seen or heard of before? Even if you give access in the case of well-known companies such as Microsoft, be sure to monitor what their representatives do every step of the way.

Downloads present one of the main security risks. There is no need to install and download any software to build and publish a website, and I was naïve to do that since that's the easiest way to get in trouble. If an open source platform wants you to download their software, do not do it and move on!

The same thing goes for your user accounts – do not give your username and password to anyone unless it's necessary and you can be sure they won't be careless or abuse it.

Know the risk of using Wi-Fi

Even if you use strong password, that won't help if a hacker intercepts it. Wi-Fi exposes you to this risk, especially when it comes to public hotspots. Serious issues with WPA2 security protocol that's been used with Wi-Fi were found in 2017 and still haven't been fixed [17].

Recommended security measures thus include avoiding public hotspots or only accessing them through a VPN service that encrypts your data [18]. You can also make your wireless internet connection at home safer by switching off the SSID broadcasting as well as turning Wi-Fi off when not using it.

Use reCAPTCHA

Google developed reCAPTCHA to prevent spam and abuse. It's commonly used in online forms to check whether the form has been accessed by a human or a bot. Use it in your contact and subscription forms whenever you can.

Unfortunately, though, reCAPTCHA is not available on some website builders (e.g. Strikingly). On WordPress and Tumblr, this depends on the theme and/or plugins. One possible solution is to use MailChimp's subscription form and enable reCAPTCHA there. The downside, though, is that MailChimp's forms often don't convert well.

Use GDPR

As a website owner, you are responsible for protecting the rights and privacy of your users too. Different countries have different laws and breaking these can be costly. If you have visitors from the EU, for instance, you'll have to comply with the EU General Data Protection Regulation (GDPR).

This means that it's your duty to inform the users about the kind of information (e.g. cookies, email addresses) you collect and for what purpose. In the case of a small writer's website, that would be a simple cookie notification as well as making it clear how the emails of your subscribers will be used (e.g. for sending a weekly newsletter).

GDRP is included as an option in most website builders and email marketing services. In order to become GDPR compliant, you'll thus only need to turn on these options in your website builder or use a plugin in WordPress.

4. HOSTING SERVICES

You'll need hosting for three different purposes: to manage your domain, to create email addresses and manage emails, and for website hosting. Not all hosting companies, however, provide all this nor do they do it in the same way. This can be quite confusing for a beginner.

Hosting services offer a wide range of domain, email, and website hosting plans. These services cater to a variety of users with different needs and budgets, and you'll need to find the best solution given your specific situation. Let's take a closer look at the most popular options.

Full hosting service

Full hosting service is what you need for full control over your domain and emails. These hosting plans let you create email addresses and subdomains as well as send and receive emails. Even the basic plans usually also include website hosting. Website hosting, however, isn't the easiest thing to deal with.

I thus suggest using a hosting service only for managing your domain and emails, and building your website on another platforms, such as a website builder that also hosts your website. Hosting companies, such as Ionos, Bluehost, or GoDaddy, to mention just a few, offer different hosting plans. The most basic and cheapest one should suffice if you are only going to use it for domain and emails.

The prices for the same kind of services, though, vary to a significant degree. You can easily end up overpaying, so it's worth taking the time to compare several hosting services, their plans, and prices before signing up. You'll find detailed instructions on how to do this later in this chapter.

Finding a reliable local hosting (depending on where you live) instead of looking for one globally, might be a good option too. As an example, I'm paying $45 for hosting per year (paid for 3 years in advance) at a local service in my country, and it would have been a lot less if I had fewer domains.

Shared / Cloud / Dedicated hosting

The most common hosting options you'll encounter are shared, cloud, and dedicated hosting. This, however, only matters if you opt for your own website hosting and are not going to use an external website platform (e.g. website builder such as Strikingly) that also hosts your website.

Shared hosting is usually the cheapest option and more than enough if you are only going to use it for domain and email hosting. But if you also need website hosting, this means that your site will be hosted on a server shared with many other websites. This can have a negative effect on its performance and security [19].

Cloud hosting is becoming an increasingly affordable and popular option for website hosting. If you opt for this option, your website will be hosted on several virtual servers. The resources thus won't be limited and affected by other users, and the website will be faster. Downtime is also less likely, since the hosting simply switches to another server in case of any issues [20].

With dedicated hosting, you'll have a whole server for yourself and won't share it with anyone else. While that's great for speed and security, it's too expensive for a small user on a budget. This would also be an overkill if you only have a simple website that doesn't have a lot of traffic.

Limited hosting service

You'll only be able to tell the limited hosting service apart from the full-hosting service by taking a good look at what they offer. Such services, for instance, don't provide email hosting. They might mention email forwarding, though, but be aware that this isn't one and the same thing.

Email forwarding only means that any emails sent to your domain-related email address will be forwarded to your other email address (such a Gmail). What you need, however, is to be able to send as well as receive messages using your email address, and you won't be able to do that with limited hosting.

Website builders – with or without hosting

Most writers don't need complex websites and you can quite easily build a nice and functional one with a website builder that comes with secure and reliable hosting. This doesn't require any special technical knowledge or maintenance on your part, which makes it a perfect choice for a beginner.

Be aware, though, that not all website builders and platforms provide website hosting. This, for instance, is one of the major differences between the two WordPress options, WordPress.com and WordPress.org. The former comes with website hosting, the latter doesn't.

WordPress.org is an open source platform for which you'll need to buy a separate website hosting plan. This is much more complicated and expensive than a simple domain and email hosting. What's more, it also presents a much greater security risk.

How to choose a good hosting service

It pays off to invest some time into comparing the offers and services since there are so many hosting companies you can choose from. Not all are equally good and reliable, so choose carefully. Switching from one hosting service to another can be complicated and will affect your website's uptime.

Finding a good hosting service can a bit of a challenge, though, especially if you don't know what features to look for and what to avoid. That's why I prepared a list of must-have features you should look for when shopping for domain and email hosting services.

If you decide to use an open source website builder such as WordPress.org, though, things will get more complicated. In that case, your website hosting service will not only have to cover everything on this list but also everything on the one you'll find in Chapter 7 *Website Builders & Blogs.*

Domain and email hosting must-have features

A good domain and email hosting service must provide:

1. 24/7 high-quality customer support (chat)
2. Full email hosting (not forwarding)
3. Domain transfer lock (for free)
4. WHOIS identity protection (for free)
5. Subdomains option (for free)
6. Addon domains option if you have more than one domain
7. Access to DNS records (cPanel is preferred)
8. Cost-efficient and affordable plans

All these features are important since they'll not only provide everything you need to manage your domain and emails but also make it possible for you to take care of things with as little hassle and as cost-efficiently as possible. Let's take a closer look at each of the items on the list.

Customer support

Test customer support service before you sign up to see how they respond. Do this during the weekends, holidays or at late hours of the night. If anything goes wrong with your domain or emails, you want to be sure that someone will take care of that asap no matter what day or time it is.

If you are a beginner, 24/7 chat support is a must because you will need help with setting things up. It's likely that you'll only have the time to work on this during the weekends or late in the day, so you need someone to be there for you. Having to wait for two days (or, in some cases even forever) for an email response to a ticket is not acceptable.

As for the phone option, the usefulness of it depends on where you live. International calls can be costly even if you use Skype. Also, certain dialects can be hard to understand. What's more, with chat, you'll have everything in writing, which can come in handy in the case of a dispute. A good company will send a copy of the chat transcript to your email.

Full e-mail hosting

As a domain owner, you want to be able to create custom email addresses based on your domain and use them for sending and receiving emails. Make sure that the hosting plan comes with POP/IMAP access so that you'll be able to securely connect your email address to mail clients, such as Outlook or Gmail. A good hosting service should also let you create numerous email addresses at no additional cost.

Domain Transfer Lock and WHOIS identity protection

Domain Transfer Lock and WHOIS protection are two important security features a good hosting service should provide for free. There are quite a few hosting companies that rip off their users by charging exorbitant fees for this, though, so avoid falling into such trap.

You might have to ask your hosting company to enable these features and then also check your domain's WHOIS EPP codes to see whether they did (mine didn't and had to be prompted) [11] – see sections *Identity and email protection* and *Domain Transfer Lock* in Chapter 3 *Privacy & Security*.

Subdomains

You never know whether you'll need more than one website at some point in the future. You might, for instance, want to offer some special services, such as online courses or membership and will need another website for the purpose.

As explained in Chapter 2 *Introduction to Domains*, you can simply create a free subdomain rather than buy and pay yearly fees for an additional domain. A good hosting service will include this option in your plan at no additional cost and will also not limit the number of subdomains you can create.

Addon Domains

If you plan on using more than one domain (in addition to any subdomains), pay attention to how many (if any) addon domains come with your plan. When you select your hosting plan, it will be tied to your main domain. A plan that lets you host and manage more than one domain will have an addon domain option.

This means that you'll be able to add domains, manage them, and use website hosting for each one of them at no additional cost. Another term you'll come across is parked domain. Parked domains are usually domains that were bought for resale and are not in use.

Access to DNS records and cPanel

DNS records is where you can point or connect your domain to a website. You'll find this section in cPanel. cPanel is a control panel where you manage domains and emails as well as create email addresses. It's easy to use and became a dashboard of choice at most hosting services. You'll find more on cPanel in Chapter 5 *Managing Domains & Emails*.

Website builders provide instructions on how to connect or point a domain to your website in cPanel, and you can even take cPanel for a test drive at the company that created it [21]. There's no reason to feel overwhelmed, though. If you'll just use a hosting service for domain and email management, you'll only need *Domains* and *Email* sections in cPanel.

Cost-efficient and affordable plans

Many hosting companies use deceptive pricing and tricks to lure you into signing up, so be careful when evaluating plans and prices. Overpriced deals camouflaged as a bargain are common. One of the regular tricks is to offer a bargain price and then state somewhere in small print that this price is only valid for the first term of hosting.

What's presented as $1.99 can thus turn into $11.99 per month as soon as the next payment is due. Pay attention to any asterisks next to the prices and specifically ask their customer service about the regular price you'll have to pay after the initial term. Also, make sure that the company doesn't charge extra for services such as privacy protection and domain lock.

Finally, see what's included in plans – what type of hosting (shared, cloud…), how many email addresses and subdomains you can create, how many addon domains you can have, and how much space you'll get on their server.

5. MANAGING DOMAINS & EMAILS

Now that you have bought a domain and chosen a hosting service and plan, it's time to start using your domain and create your new email address. To do this, you'll have to become familiar with cPanel and learn how to use it.

Create a new email address

Creating an email address in cPanel is one of the easiest things to do. Just go to the *Email* section on your cPanel, click *Email Accounts*, and then select *Add Email Account* [22]. Put in the desired name in the *Email* field (this will be the field before the @your-domain.com part) and then select a domain in the *Domain* field (e.g. your-domain.com).

Now you will also have to set up your password. Make sure you create a strong password that cannot be easily cracked (refer to *Passwords* section in Chapter 12 *Useful Apps & Tools*). Copy and save this password somewhere where you'll be able to find it later, for you'll need it for setting up your mail client (e.g. an app such as Outlook or Gmail).

Finally, click *Create Account*. That's it, your new email address is ready. Now you only need to set up your mail client so that you can start sending and receiving emails.

Managing emails

You can get access to your emails in two ways – through webmail at your hosting service or by configuring your mail client. You'll need to use webmail occasionally to get rid of spam or emails that could pose a security threat. Your mail client might warn you about these and leave them on your hosting service's server. In such cases, you'll have to use webmail to access and delete such messages.

Webmail

The best way to access your webmail is through cPanel. Go to the *Email* section in the cPlanel, select *Email Accounts*, and then click *Access Webmail* next to your email address. You'll see the three webmail apps you can choose from – Horde, Roundcube, and SquirrelMail.

I find Horde the easiest option if you want to get rid of unwanted messages. Simply right-click the message and blacklist the sender. Then drag the message to Spam folder. Apart from that, webmail isn't a good option for a normal day-to-day use, and it's far better to configure a mail client.

Configuring Mail Client

Mail client is an email application, such as Outlook or Gmail you might already use. You can connect your new email address to any of such apps. Some apps, such as Outlook, offer an automatic set-up, but do not use that. Set up your account manually instead, so that you can enable SSL.

I'm including detailed instructions on how to do this for Outlook and Gmail here. This works similarly on all such apps, so you might be able to use these instructions for other mail clients too. You can also look for the instructions in the *Email Accounts* section of cPanel, your hosting service's Help section, or in the mail client's Help section.

Using Outlook as your mail client

Go to Outlook, click File and look for the tiny *Add Account* option just below the *Account Information*. Clicking that will open a pop-up window. Insert the email address you'd like to connect and click *Advanced options* beneath it. Make sure to check *Let me set up my account manually*.

Select *POP* among the options you'll see. This will open *POP Account Settings*. Start by setting up *Incoming mail*. In the *Server* bar, insert your server's email address. This is usually your domain's subdomain "mail," e.g. mail.your-domain.com. In my case, that's mail.matejaklaric.com.

To set up your account securely using SSL, use port 995 and check "This server requires an encrypted connection (SSL/TLS)." You will also see the *Secure Password Authentication* option but unless your hosting service requires it (most don't) leave it unchecked. You have now set up everything you need to securely receive emails.

The next step is to set this up for sending emails as well. In the same pop-up window, you'll find *Outgoing mail* section. Use the same mail.your-domain.com server you used before. This time, though, the port should be 465 and the selected *Encryption method* should be SSL/TLS. Again, don't use the *Secure Password Authentication* unless your hosting service requires it.

When done, click *Next*. This will prompt you to insert your email address password – that's the password you set up at your hosting service when creating your email address. Insert it and click *Connect*. When done, test your new email account by sending a test email from your new email address to another email address and vice versa.

Finally, make sure that your emails get transferred from your hosting service's server to Outlook, so that they won't remain on the server and clutter your webmail. To check for that, click *File* on the top menu in Outlook and select *Account Settings* under the *Account Information*. Now click *Account Settings* at the top of the drop-down menu and then select your new email account so that it's highlighted.

Next, click *Change* on the menu above the email. This will open another pop-up window where you'll find *Mail settings* and the option to leave the messages on the server. Either deselect this altogether or make sure to select the option to delete these messages from the server after a certain number of days or when you delete them in Outlook.

Using Gmail as your mail client

If you already use Gmail for your personal emails, it would make sense to use it as your mail client as well. This solution is very convenient, since you'll be able to manage the emails from both private and professional email accounts using the same mailbox.

When you'll get an email message, you'll see to which email address it was sent to (e.g. personal or professional) and will be able to respond using appropriate email address. You'll also be able to set up email signatures and automated responses for each of these email addresses separately.

Setting Gmail as your mail client is a bit more complicated than Outlook, though, since you have to set it up for sending and receiving emails in two separate steps. The following instructions will make this easier for you. Let's start by setting your Gmail account for sending emails.

Gmail settings for sending emails:

1. Click the *Settings* (gear) icon under your profile picture in Gmail and select *Settings* from the drop-down menu.
2. Click *Accounts and Imports* from the top menu.
3. Scroll down to *Send mail as* and click *Add another email address*.
4. This will open a pop-up window. Here, enter the name and email address you'd like to use for sending emails.
5. Select *Treat as an alias* and click *Next Step*.
6. Now, you'll have to insert your mail server information: *SMPT Server* (e.g. mail.your-domain.com. In my case, for instance, that's mail.matejaklaric.com), *Port* (Use 465 for secure SSL connection), *Username* (This would be your new email address), *Password* (Password you set up when creating this email address at your hosting service).
7. Make sure to select *Secured connection using SSL*.
8. Click *Save Changes*.

You should now be able to send messages using your new email address. The next step is to set up Gmail so that you can receive messages as well.

Gmail settings for receiving emails:

1. Still in the main *Accounts and Imports* dashboard, scroll down to the *Check email from other accounts* and click *Add an email account*.
2. This will again open a pop-up window. Here, enter your new email address.
3. Like before, you'll have to use your mail server information: *Username* (That would be your new email address), *Password* (The password you set up when

41

creating this email address at your hosting service), **POP server** (e.g. mail.your-domain.com. In my case, for instance, that's mail.matejaklaric.com), and **Port** (e.g. 995 for secure SSL connection).

4. Make sure to select **Always use a secure connection (SSL) when retrieving mail**.
5. Do **NOT** select **Leave a copy of retrieved message on the server** – if you do, all the emails will also remain on your hosting service's server. This will lead to clutter and take up your limited disk space, and you'll have to keep deleting these emails manually in webmail.
6. Click **Save Changes**.

There is one last step you need to take – before you can start using Gmail as your mail client, you'll have to confirm your request. Gmail will send an email to your new email address and you'll have to access it through webmail at your hosting service (refer to the *Webmail* section earlier in this chapter). Only after you confirm that, will any new emails be sent through to your Gmail account. This is the confirmation email:

You have requested to add [your new email] to your Gmail account.

Confirmation code: [you will see the number here]

Before you can send mail from [your new email] using your Gmail account, please click the link below to confirm your request: [this is where you'll see the link].

If you click the link and it appears to be broken, please copy and paste it into a new browser window.

If you aren't able to access the link, please log in to your Gmail account and click 'Settings' at the top of any page. Open the 'Accounts' tab and locate the email address you'd like to add in the 'Send mail as:' section. Then, click 'Verify' and enter your confirmation code: [here you will see the same number again].

Thanks for using Gmail!

After you confirmed your request either by clicking the link or using the verification code, test whether everything works as it should have – send an email from another email account to your new email address and vice versa. If you did everything right, this should work both ways. If not, contact your domain hosting service and ask for help.

Be aware, though, that it can take some time before you receive messages in your Gmail mailbox. You can speed up the process by manually checking for new emails. To do that, go to *Accounts & Imports* dashboard again, scroll down to *Check email from other accounts* and click *Check mail now* next to your email address.

Domain and DNS settings

Now that you took care of your emails, it's time to learn how to use cPanel for redirecting or pointing (connecting) your domain and creating subdomains. For these options, you'll use the *Domains* section in your cPanel. That's where you'll find *DNS Zone Editor*, *Redirects*, and *Subdomains*.

DNS Zone Editor

You'll need *DNS Zone Editor* for connecting a domain to your website or blog. DNS stands for Domain Name System and it includes *A Record* and *CNAME Record* options, which is what you need. How exactly you'll have to do that, though, depends on your website builder or blogging platform. They will give you specific instructions.

To get access to A and CNAME records, go to *DNS Zone Editor* and click *Manage* next to your domain. This will open a dashboard in which you'll see zone records for your domain. That's where you can edit or add a record.

Pointing or connecting a domain

Both A records and CNAME records can be used to connect or point a domain to a website. If, for instance, you created a blog on Tumblr and want to connect your domain to it, use A record and point it to the IP address of Tumblr's server. Then set up CNAME record for the www version of your domain so that both naked and www domain versions load the blog [23].

If you, however, use an open source platform such as WordPress.org, you'll have to point A record to your website hosting server's IP address since that's where your site will be hosted. With website builder Strikingly, on the other hand, you won't need A record, but will have to create a www redirect and then set up a CNAME record instead.

As you can see, website platforms do this in all sorts of ways. To add to the confusion, their instructions are often also not exactly clear. You might have to ask your domain hosting service for help with this, and that's where it will become clear why it's so important to choose a hosting company with a good, competent, and responsive customer service.

If you use website builder Strikingly, their customer support can also set this up for you [24]. They will need access to your domain hosting account, though, so make sure to change the password afterwards.

DNS propagation

After you took care of the DNS settings, it will take a while for that to propagate. Propagation means that the servers all over the world need to update their records so that your website's URL becomes associated with your new DNS settings. This is what makes it possible for your website to load [25].

Propagation can take anywhere from an hour to a couple of days. Waiting for this can be frustrating, especially if you are not sure whether you've done everything correctly. With services such as Global DNS Propagation Checker, however, you can monitor the propagation in real-time as well as check whether the settings lead to where they are supposed to [26].

Redirecting (forwarding) a domain

Redirecting (also known as forwarding) a domain can be useful in two cases. First, when you don't have a website yet and thus want to redirect your domain to a temporary landing page (you'll find more on this in Chapter 6 *Landing Pages*).

And second, you can use a redirect to set-up either www or naked domain as your preferred (canonical) URL. Be aware though, that you can only do this in some cases, since this has a lot to do with the settings at your website hosting service and the system they use.

Creating a redirect

Creating a redirect is very easy. Go to the *Domains* section of the cPanel and click *Redirect*. Now select Permanent (301) redirect and select your domain from the drop-down menu. Then insert the URL of the site to where your want to redirect your domain to.

It's recommended (for SEO reasons) that you always use Permanent (301) redirect instead of Temporary (302) option even if you are only temporarily redirecting to a landing page [27]. Also, be careful with www and no-www options.

In case that you are redirecting to a landing page, select "Redirect with or without www." If, however, you are setting up a redirect to www domain (e.g. in the case of Strikingly), choose "Do Not Redirect www." In both cases, don't select Wild Card Redirect. Click "Add" and you're done.

Creating subdomains

To create a subdomain, go to the *Domains* sections in cPanel and click *Subdomains*. Insert the subdomain name (e.g. "courses," "members" or "blog") and select a domain from which you'd like to create the subdomain. For my website, for instance, I created a subdomain members.matejaklaric.com. When done, click *Create*.

To point or connect your subdomain to a website, go to the *DNS Editor* in the *Domains* section of your c Panel, and click *Manage* next to the domain you used to create the subdomain. You'll find your new subdomain in the main domain's DNS records. There, you can set up its A or CNAME record just like you did for the main domain.

6. LANDING PAGES

Landing pages are simple one-page websites that can be used for various purposes, such a promoting a new product, growing an email list, or as a replacement for your website.

Creating a simple landing page is much faster and easier than building a website, so you can use it as a temporary solution while taking the time to create a permanent website. It's easy to redirect or connect your domain to a landing page and there are different approaches you can use, for instance:

- Set up your **author page** on Amazon, Books2Read, or BookBub and redirect your domain to it.
- Use a **website builder** to build a simple landing page and connect your domain to it.
- Use **email marketing service**, such as MailerLite that has a landing page option and connect your domain to it.

The benefits of using your author page on Amazon, BookBub, or Books2Read are that you likely already have one, they promote your books, look professional, are free and secure, and it's very easy to redirect your domain to them. That would be the fastest and easiest solution.

Another option is to build a landing page using a website builder. This too can be a good temporary solution since you can create and launch a simple coming-soon landing page in a matter of hours. The benefit of this option is that you can use a subscription form to get new subscribers, especially if you offer an incentive, such as a free ebook.

Make sure, though, to also use a call-to-action, such as "Subscribe to be notified when I launch" or "Sign-up for a free ebook." The problem with this option, however, might be SSL certificate. You can usually only get one on paid plans, and this may be expensive and thus not cost-efficient.

As the third option, you can use an email marketing service and create your page there. MailerLite, for instance, have a nice and easy-to-use landing page builder. To be able to connect your domain and get SSL certificate, though, you'll need their paid plan, but at least this will cover both the landing page and email marketing.

Another useful alternative to these options would be to temporarily redirect your domain to your existing blog or social media account.

7. WEBSITE BUILDERS & BLOGS

In this chapter, you'll find tips on how to choose a good website builder or blog platform for a writer. It might surprise you that I don't recommend some of the most popular ones, such as Weebly, Wix, and Squarespace. Among the main reasons for this is that they aren't supported on certain Android in-built browsers.

Given the Android's enormous popularity and the fact that it's by far the most used OS for mobile devices in the world, opting for a website builder that is not well-supported on its browsers is not a good idea. This is even more true at the time when people prefer to browse using their mobile devices, and this trend just keeps growing.

Browser issues, though, are not the only reason why I excluded so many platforms. Just like for hosting services, I created a list of must-have features for website builders and blog platforms. Those who failed to deliver in the most important areas didn't make it into this book. The ones that made it are WordPress, Strikingly, Tumblr, and IM Creator.

I included the last two options because they might be a good choice for those who cannot afford to spend much if anything on a website. Both Tumblr and IM Creator will host your blog or website and let you connect your custom domain for free, and this includes SSL certificate.

Must-have features

If you choose to go with a website builder, make sure it provides everything on the must-have features list below. If you, however, plan on using an open source or blog platform (e.g. WordPress or Tumblr), things will, yet again, get a bit more complicated.

In that case, some of the items on this list will have to be taken care of by your domain hosting service, while others will be the matter of the themes and plugins you'll get from external developers. You'll find more on this in *WordPress* and *Tumblr* sections later in this chapter.

Website hosting must-have features:

1. 24/7 high-quality customer support (chat)
2. The option to connect your custom domain
3. Free SSL certificate
4. Reliability (uptime) and speed
5. AMP technology
6. Responsive themes
7. Supported across devices and browsers
8. User-friendly interface
9. Well-designed themes
10. Blog option
11. Integrations (social media, Google Analytics…)
12. Subscription forms
13. Cost-efficient and affordable plans

Let's take a closer look at each of these features.

Customer support

The one thing on the very top of the list is, again, a high-quality 24/7 customer support. As suggested earlier, do test this before you sign up. Your website is a property and the more time and money you'll invest in it, the greater the loss if anything goes wrong.

This is not just about getting timely help and support in case that your site goes down or there are any problems, though. You will likely already need help while building your website. Be aware that in the case that you buy a premium theme for Tumblr or WordPress, the developer who created it will have to provide this support as well.

Free SSL certificate

As explained earlier, if your website hosting doesn't come with an SSL certificate, your website won't be displayed through a safe protocol. This not only looks unprofessional and leads to a red safety warning displayed next to your URL but also lowers the website's ranking in search results. Make sure SSL comes with your plan.

Reliability (uptime) and speed

Uptime and speed are two major factors that can damage your site's popularity and ranking. Speed indicates how fast your website loads. Ideally, this would take less than 3 seconds, but according to Google, 70% of websites don't load that fast or at least not on mobile devices [28].

The faster your website loads, the more likely it is that the visitors won't abandon it before they even see it. Your website's speed will depend on the website hosting service (e.g. website builder or blogging platform) as well as your own errors (e.g. using too large images).

Good platforms apply technical solutions to increase the speed, such as compressing the images and lazy loading. Lazy loading is used by some website builders (for instance, Strikingly) because it increases the website's speed by only displaying the images that fall inside the screen as the visitor scrolls instead of loading the whole website at once. You can also use lazy loading on WordPress, but you'll have to get a plugin for that.

Uptime of your website is another important factor. It's expressed as a percent and signifies how often is your website down. This could happen due to technical issues or maintenance. The perfect uptime would be 100% or as close to that as possible.

Differently from dedicated website hosting services, website builders as a rule don't mention the uptime you can expect. In any case, though, you'll only get a reliable insight into the uptime of your website by regularly monitoring it with apps, such as Uptime Robot [29].

AMP (Accelerated Mobile Pages) technology

Give preference to website builders and themes that use AMP (Accelerated Mobile Pages) technology since this is the technology for mobile devices recommended by Google [30]. Using it will have a positive impact on your SEO and website ranking (you'll learn more about SEO in Chapter 11 *SEO & Google*).

Strikingly uses AMP and so does Tumblr, but it might not work with all Tumblr's themes, so you'll have to check for that before you buy the theme. In WordPress, you'll have to look for themes that are AMP ready. IM Creator doesn't make it clear whether they use this technology or not.

Responsive themes

Responsive themes adapt and look good on any type of screen. They were created to perform well on mobile devices where non-responsive themes failed to deliver satisfactory results. Since most people nowadays use mobile devices for browsing, Google started to evaluate websites and set their ranking based on mobile performance. Responsive themes are thus a must, so make sure you get one.

Support across devices and browsers

If your website won't load or has technical issues on some browsers, that's a big problem. For some reason, website builders often fail to disclose this information and unless you use one of the unsupported browsers yourself, you might not even be aware that there is an issue.

That's why I recommend using Google Analytics that can help you detect any such issues (you'll find more on that in *Google Analytics* section in Chapter 11 *SEO & Google*). Such problems usually occur on mobile browsers. For a start, you can test website platforms' homepages by trying to access them using different browsers and devices.

If the website builder's homepage loads across the browsers and devices with no issues, you can expect the same for your website. With blog platforms, though, this will also depend on the theme, so you'll have to check each of the ones you consider buying as well.

User-friendly interface

Not every website builder has a user-friendly interface, and some are so complicated that you end up spending weeks trying to figure things out (e.g. WordPress.org). Nowadays, though, there is no need for this since it's quite easy to create a website with a good website builder. Give a platform a try before you buy to check the interface.

Well-designed themes

There are many website builders and developers, but not all of them have good themes. Either these aren't designed well or have technical issues. Especially with WordPress and Tumblr themes, take the time to go thoroughly test the ones that look promising. Also, make sure that they don't just look good, but also come with all the must-have features you need.

Blog option

For a writer, having a blog is a must. That's one of the best ways to showcase your writing, get new subscribers, and communicate with your audience. Google will rank your website based on content too, and you can get a lot of organic and social media traffic from blog posts and stories.

Integrations (social media, Google Analytics)

Social media integrations help you grow your following and encourage sharing. At the very least, the theme should have social media icons as well as social share option in your blog posts. If it also has a social media gallery, that's a bonus since this helps you promote your latest posts.

Another important integration any good platform should have is Google Analytics. If you use it, you'll get access to crucial information regarding your website's performance. (you'll find more on this in Chapter 11 *SEO & Google*).

Integration with MailChimp (or any other email marketing service you use) would be a bonus too. This, however, is not necessary until you start getting a lot of subscribers. Such integrations automatically sync new subscribers' emails with your email list, so that you don't have to do it manually.

Subscription forms

Embedded subscription forms are another must-have feature. The best website builders will not only let you place one on your website but will also automatically add it to the end of every blog post (Strikingly does that). This improves the form's conversion rate since it's more likely that a reader will subscribe after reading a story or post they enjoyed.

Cost-efficient and affordable plans

Like with hosting services, what might initially seem like a good price can soon turn out to be anything but great. Check which features are included in your plan or theme to make sure you'll get everything you need. Be even more careful with open source platforms such as WordPress.com, for you may end up paying a lot more than expected. Good themes and plugins are expensive, and the costs add up quickly.

8. THE PLATFORMS – PROS & CONS

Now that you know what to look for, it's time to take a closer look at the platforms, consider their pros and cons, and see how they fare against each other.

WordPress

The advice commonly given to writers regarding websites is to use WordPress. I cannot, however, in the least agree with that. While this might have been true years ago, I don't think this is still the best option for a writer who isn't tech savvy, is chronically short on time and money, and doesn't need a terribly complex website.

I don't use WordPress since it's too complicated and costly, especially if you want a good theme with all the must-have features. Also, there are major differences between the two WordPress options. Creating and running a website on WordPress.org is very different from using WordPress.com. If you choose WordPress, you need to know the difference.

WordPress.com

If you mainly want to blog, aren't a developer, can afford to pay a rather steep price, and don't have much time for maintenance and hosting, WordPress.com could be a good option. WordPress.com is a user-friendly sister platform to WordPress.org, and its main benefit is that it includes website hosting and 24/7 customer support (chat).

This, however, is above all a blogging platform, and its free plan doesn't have enough features to be of much use. Comparing to WordPress.org and website builders, it thus offers less when it comes to functionality and design. Given what you get, the price is high. In order to be rid of WordPress ads and get access to the must-have features, you'll have to opt for a Business plan. Plus, you'll still need to buy plugins to get the website to where it needs to be.

Pros

- Secure website hosting.
- Free SSL certificate on all plans.
- 24/7 chat support.
- Custom domains on paid plans.
- AMP technology for mobile devices.
- Backups are taken care of by the platform.
- Manual backup option is also available.
- Optimized for blogging.

Cons

- No custom domain on the free plan.
- You'll have to buy a yearly plan straight away to be able to start building a website.
- Pricy if you want the must-have features and access to unlimited premium themes.
- You have to buy plugins for full-functionality.
- You need Business plan to be able to install plugins.
- Not all plugins are allowed, and you'll have to check the list of incompatible ones to see what you can do [31].
- You don't get access to emails of your blog's followers if they subscribed using their WordPress.com account.

WordPress.org

Running your website on WordPress.org requires a good website hosting that is complicated to set-up and maintain. On the other hand, though, the platform also gives you many more options and you can use it to build more complex and demanding websites for all sorts of purposes.

The website hosting for this, however, is not nearly as simple and affordable as is a simple domain and email hosting. Good WordPress hosting services are anything but cheap and start at about $30 per month at the lower end [32]. Most hosting companies charge for this once per year and you'll have to pay for 12 months upfront.

Also consider that you'll have to learn how to properly manage website hosting, use WordPress builder and themes, deal with security issues and backups as well as choose among a myriad of plugins. You'll also have to keep all this regularly updated and this can lead to some unexpected and unwelcome results.

Unless you are a developer, you probably don't want to deal with all this and especially not on a regular basis. The last thing you need is constant worrying about security, updates, and whether everything has been taken of properly.

What's worse, there is no dedicated customer support on WordPress.org since it's an open source platform. While this means that the platform is free to use, it also means that you are on your own. Also, when you add up the cost of hosting, premium themes, and plugins, it turns out that this is one of the most expensive rather than a free option.

One of the most disturbing issues with WordPress.org, however, is security. WordPress is the most hacked website platform in the world, and that's something you need to be aware of if you decide to use it [33].

Pros

- You can build a unique and complex website.
- A variety of plugins give you numerous options.
- Great if can afford high-quality website hosting plan, are tech savvy or can hire someone to manage it for you.

Cons

- You'll need to use an external hosting service to set up and manage your website.
- You'll have to pay for the more expensive website hosting plan, themes, and plugins straight away to be able to start building your website.
- You'll have to acquire and install SSL certificate at your website hosting service.
- No dedicated customer support beyond the support of your hosting service.
- You'll need to buy premium themes and external plugins for full-functionality, security, and speed.
- You'll have to deal with different customer service for every theme and plugin you use, for these are developed by different companies and developers.
- Security risk is higher.
- You'll have to take care of backups, plugins, and theme updates regularly.
- Technical and security issues can be caused by plugins, themes, and old or missing updates.
- Setting everything up is time-consuming and complicated.

Strikingly

Strikingly is a website builder I use since it delivers everything on the must-have features list. There are some issues and downsides too, but the benefits nevertheless outweigh these. Strikingly is a good choice for a beginner since it's easy to use and offers 24/7 chat support, good themes, and useful features. You can create a nice and functional website there quite easily.

One of the major downsides, though, is that it only has a simple and basic blog. By far the worst part of this is that the user loses access to the menu and cannot see the title of the website when they open a blog post. Since people often land on a website through the links to blog posts, that's a major problem. If the visitors don't see the website's title, they have no idea on whose website they even are.

Strikingly is nevertheless a nice option for great-looking landing pages and websites. You can build a free website too, but that doesn't come with an SSL certificate and has limited options. You'll have to invest in Pro plan to get access to everything on the must-have list.

The pricing, though, is competitive and even generous if you need more than one website, for Strikingly lets you create three premium sites on Pro plan.

Pros

- Secure website hosting.
- SSL certificate on paid plans.
- 24/7 chat support.
- Custom domains on paid plans.
- AMP technology for mobile devices.
- Uses lazy loading technique to speed up the site.

- Backup restore available for up to the last 8-10 changes.
- Responsive themes.
- User-friendly interface.
- Good pricing if you need more than one website.
- You can already do a lot of work on a free trial plan so that you won't have to start paying straight away.
- You can opt for monthly or yearly payments.
- You'll get access to emails of the followers of your blog.

Cons

- Simplified blog option with limited features.
- The menu and website title disappear in open blog posts.
- You can only add one button per section.
- No SSL on free plans.
- No custom domain on free plans.
- No reCAPTCHA option for forms.

IM Creator (IM XPRS)

IM Creator, formerly known as IM XPRS, offers one free website with premium features to creators (writers too), and that's the main reason why I included it. Another is that you can create quite impressive websites even though the interface isn't as intuitive and easy to use as Strikingly

A major downside of IM Creator, however, is their customer support. There is no 24/7 chat option, so you'll have to submit a ticket and wait. It can take a day or two before you get a response and that's why I wouldn't recommend it unless you only need a landing page or are broke.

If you are on a tight budget, though, it might be worth giving it a try. Just one tip, though – if a representative tells you that you cannot get a free SSL certificate with your free premium website for creators, send them this link https://www.sslforfree.com/ (SSL for free) and ask them if they could enable it for you.

I used IM Creator to build a landing page for my book *The Story of the Fox and White Rabbit: Not Your Ordinary Fable*: https://www.the-fox-and-white-rabbit.com/.

Pros

- Secure website hosting.
- SSL certificate on paid plans.
- 24/7 chat support.
- Custom domains on paid plans.
- Responsive themes.
- Free premium websites for creators (including custom domain and SSL certificate).
- You can add multiple buttons per section (useful for giving links to various online bookstores).
- Impressive effects and transitions.
- Great design options.

Cons

- No 24/7 chat customer support, only tickets.
- No SSL on free websites.
- Blog leaves much to be desired.
- Dysfunctional links on the dashboard (the links to support and help sections are broken).
- Hard to find their contact form or email.
- Help sections are outdated (you'll have to google to find what you need).

- SSL is available only on www domain and https:// with naked domain won't even load your website (the only platform of the ones in this book with this issue).
- Once you choose a template, you'll be stuck with it unless you contact customer support and ask them to change it.
- No reCAPTCHA option for forms.

Tumblr

Tumblr is another good option if you are on a tight budget and your main goal is blogging. It's a blogging platform that also functions as a community of users, similarly to social media. Tumblr is free to use, comes with SSL certificate, uses AMP technology for mobile devices, and you can also connect a custom domain to your blog for free.

You can even create several separate sub-blogs in addition to your main blog, connect all of them to custom domains, and manage them using the same account. At the end of 2018, Tumblr also banned all adult content from the platform. This may be bad for those who are interested in porn but is good for everyone else since it now makes Tumblr suitable for all types of audiences.

The main downside of Tumblr, though, is their poor customer support. There is no 24/7 chat option, so you are left at the mercy of their ticket system. If anything goes wrong, it can take days for them to respond let alone solve the issue, and it's not uncommon to not hear back from them at all [34]. This is where you get what you pay for.

Another thing are their themes. The official Tumblr theme is free to use, looks nice, and it's sure to deliver when it comes to SSL certificate and AMP mobile technology (you can turn it on in the advance options). But if you want the rest of the features on the must-have list, you'll have to find and buy a good premium theme, and that can be a challenge.

The main benefit of buying a Tumblr theme is that you'll only have to pay once for a lifetime use. At around $50 per theme, that's an affordable option. On the downside, though, you'll have to sieve through a bunch of themes with different functionalities that were created by different developers. Not all developers provide decent customer support and if there are any issues with these themes, Tumblr support will likely not be able to help you.

The recommended approach to buying premium themes is to check the developer and their website for customer support options before buying. Then contact them with a few questions regarding the theme you are interested in. The kind of response (or the lack of it) will be a good indicator of what you can expect as their customer.

I use Tumblr for a couple of my less important domains. While I haven't tested every single developer and theme, I tried a few. Based on their themes and outstanding customer support, Precrafted might be a good option [35].

Finally, due to the Tumblr's concept that combines social media approach with blogging platform, it takes a while before you get familiar with how everything works. Tumblr is not the simplest platform of them all, and you'll have to learn how to install and manage themes [36].

Pros

- Free for all – no paid plans.
- Secure website hosting.
- SSL certificate on all blogs.
- Custom domains on all blogs.
- AMP technology for mobile devices.

- You can create additional blogs using the same account
- Nice and responsive official theme
- Premium themes are highly affordable.
- Good for blogging.

Cons

- No 24/7 chat customer support, only tickets.
- Limited functionality of the official theme.
- Limited options even with premium themes.
- Premium themes can have inadequate or no support.
- Time-consuming when it comes to setting everything up and learning how to use the platform.
- You don't get access to emails of your followers.

9. HOW TO CHOOSE A PLATFORM

Now that you are familiar with the main pros and cons of different platforms, it's time to decide which one would be best given your goals. This decision shouldn't be taken lightly, and it might be a good idea to take at least some of the options for a test drive. Start by taking the following into account:

- Your budget, including recurring costs
- Time needed to set it up and maintain
- Your goals and needs
- Security

The perfect choice won't break your budget, won't take more time than you can afford to spend on it, will suit your goals and needs, and will provide a comfortable level of security.

Budget

When considering your budget, don't forget counting in any additional expenses. Website builders, for instance, come at a fixed price with no additional costs, while open source platforms require hosting as well as plugins and themes. Make a list of all the expenses and compare the options:

- Domain (recurring payments)
- Domain and email hosting (recurring payments)
- Website hosting or website builder (recurring payments)
- Blog platform (free or recurring payments)
- Theme, including updates and support (free, one-time, or recurring payments)

- Plugins, including updates and support (free, one-time, or recurring payments)

Now calculate the costs for each platform and consider your goals and needs. This will not be the same for everyone. What works for me might not work for you, but I'll show you how I went about this just to give you an example.

Website builders

The two builders I use are Strikingly and IM Creator. Here's is how I calculated the cost per website based on my needs:

Strikingly

I need more than one website, and since Strikingly Pro plan let me build three premium websites on one plan, I created three of my websites there. The costs, including hosting, domains, and running the website, thus are:

- Domains: $10 per domain per year (will be $15 each next year)
- Domain and email hosting: $45 total per year
- Strikingly, monthly payments: $240 per year for three websites.

Strikingly is a securely hosted website builder that comes with all the features I need, so I don't need to buy anything else. The end cost for my main writer's website matejaklaric.com, including the domain and hosting for all of my domains, is thus $135 per year.

Another premium site I created on the same Pro plan is a landing page for my website for members, and I connected a subdomain to it. Since I can create free subdomains on my domain hosting plan, that came at no additional expense. The final cost for my members.matejaklaric.com website is thus $80 per year.

As a transformation guide, I also created *Transform the Pain* as the third website on the same plan. I use a domain transformthepain.com for it, which makes the final cost slightly higher due to the yearly fee for the domain. My hosting plan, though, includes free addon domains, so there's no additional cost for hosting. Yearly cost for this site is thus $90.

The final cost for running all three premium websites on Strikingly, including domain and email hosting, is a bit over $300 per year and my average cost per website on Strikingly is thus about $100 per year.

IM Creator (IM XPRS)

I'm currently using IM Creator for a landing page for my book *The Story of the Fox and White Rabbit* [37]. It comes with custom domain, SSL certificate, and other premium features. Since the website is hosted for free and I added the domain to my domain hosting plan at no additional cost, I only pay a yearly fee for the domain.

The website on IM Creator thus costs me $10 per year – a yearly fee for the domain. If this were my only website, though, I'd have to add the cost of domain hosting to this too. The total in that case would be $50 per year.

WordPress

Give the popularity of WordPress, I gave both WordPress.org and WordPress.com a try. They, however, were too pricy and not best suited for my needs. If you only need a blog, this might be a good option. Since I have several websites and landing pages, though, this was far from the most cost-efficient solution for me.

WordPress.com

For roughly the same functionality and must-have features I have on Strikingly, I'd have to opt for a Business plan on WordPress.com and then also buy at least one premium plugin. That would cost me well over $300 per year for a single website. This means that I'd have to pay well over $900 per year to run the three sites I now have on Strikingly.

Add to this the cost of domain and email hosting, and you get to well over $1,000 for three websites. Now compare over $330 per website to $100 on Strikingly and you'll see how easy it was for me to drop WordPress. What's more, there is no monthly payment option on WordPress.com and if you are on a tight budget, coming up with that much money upfront alone can be an issue.

On the other hand, though, a blog on WordPress.com is better than the one I have on Strikingly. Whether that's worth the price will depend on your budget, goals, and needs. You might also be tempted to choose a lower priced plan on WordPress.com but be warned that these plans don't come with the must-have features you need.

WordPress.org

The cost of WordPress.org is much harder to calculate since it depends on so many factors – there is a hosting service with a website hosting plan, and then the themes, plugins, storage, backup, and security options. The price for a single website on WordPress.org with all the must-have features and adequate level of security can range from about $400 at the lowest end to several thousand dollars per year [38].

Tumblr

If you connect custom domain to your blog and use the official Tumblr theme, you'll get a website for free. This, however, will not give you most of the must-have features. To get those, you'll have to buy one of the premium themes, and the ones with most features usually cost around $50.

I currently use Tumblr as a temporary solution for the *Self-Publishing Made Easy* website and have connected it to my custom domain self-publishing-made-easy.com. I added this domain to my hosting plan at no additional cost and chose a simple $19 theme (affordable, but it doesn't have all the must-have features). This was a one-time payment, so the yearly cost for this website is now $10 for the domain fee.

Time and maintenance

Most freelancers and writers are already overburdened and have little time to spare. Base your decision on how much time you can realistically spend on creating and regularly maintaining your website too. When calculating the time needed, consider that some platforms are more user-friendly than others and they make everything faster and easier.

Among the options presented in this book, WordPress.org takes by far the most time for the initial setup as well as managing the website. Tumblr is also not the easiest one to figure out. WordPress.com, as another option, comes with hosting so it will be easier to set it up, but you'll still need to find the right theme and plugins.

Just choosing, testing, and finding the best theme and plugins can be time-consuming and draining, since there are so many that vary significantly in features, customer support, and pricing. This goes for Tumblr as well.

Strikingly was the least time-consuming option for me. They have a limited but nice selection of themes and a user-friendly interface. Customer support service is there 24/7 and if something happens, you can simply report the issue and they'll take care of it.

Goals and needs

Once you have a better idea of what you can do with each of these platforms, how much they cost, and how much time each of them takes, consider which of them would also help you achieve the most.

I, for instance, use these platforms for different purposes. The best choice will thus not only depend on your budget and time but also on what you want to achieve. Here is a list of possible goals you might have regarding your website:

- grow your following,
- build your audience,
- promote your books,
- blog and showcase your writing,
- make it easy for people to connect with you,
- use it as an info point,
- use it as a membership platform.

Your goals might encompass everything on this list, parts of it, or something else that's not on the list. Given these goals, figure out which platform would be best for what you want to do. If you want to grow your email list, you'll need access to the email addresses of people who subscribed and follow your blog.

While building the following on WordPress.com and Tumblr is a good thing, these platforms won't give you access to the emails of your followers. You'll thus have to figure out how to convince people to also subscribe and not just follow you. On Strikingly, however, you'll get access to the emails of everyone who follows your blog.

As another example, if you only want to promote your new book, a nice landing page could be perfectly enough. For that, you certainly don't need WordPress's $300 Business plan.

Security

While security is important, it can be more important in some cases than others. In the case of a landing page, for instance, if it goes down for days, that won't be nearly as bad as if that happened to your main website after you invested months of your time and hundreds of dollars into it.

For less important projects or temporary solutions, it's less risky to run your website, blog, or a landing page on a platform that doesn't come with 24/7 customer support. Even though it might take several days for the platform to take care of any issues, you can simply disconnect and redirect your domain until the problem gets solved.

You shouldn't risk having your main website down for hours let alone days, though. Consider that you'll publish and promote the link to your main website everywhere – your books, social media accounts, promos, and ads. Whenever your website goes down, you are losing on your investment and that's not worth the risk.

Also, as a matter of courtesy and professionalism, you should make your site secure for those who subscribe and submit their emails or other personal information through your website. That's why you should never use platforms or plans that are not secure and don't use SSL certificates.

Final decision

Especially if you are on a tight budget, you'll likely have to sacrifice something and compromise. In the case of Tumblr and IM Creator, for instance, that will be customer support. This makes your website more vulnerable and it will take more time to get help when you need it.

If you opt for a website builder such as Strikingly or IM Creator, your blog won't be as great as it could have been on WordPress. Even though Strikingly has a much better blog than IM Creator, none of these two platforms were primarily made for blogging, while WordPress was.

If your main goal is blogging, WordPress.com might thus be the best option, but only if you can afford it. Even if you can afford it, though, it might not be the most cost-efficient solution. Tumblr would be a good blogging alternative for those on a tiny budget.

As yet another option, you can also create a simple website as an info point and then use a free platform, such as Medium, for blogging. The bottom line is that you'll have to make the final decision based on what you can afford and what you are willing to sacrifice.

10. BUILDING YOUR WEBSITE

After choosing a platform and setting your goals, the time has finally come to design and build your website. Here are a few things you'll have to consider in the process:

- One-page vs. multi-page website option
- Content
- UX and design

One-page website

Building a one-page website is by far the easiest option for a beginner. It's usually also more than enough if you just need a simple author website where you can present a couple of books, tell visitors more about yourself, and make it easy for people to connect with you.

One-page website shouldn't be confused with a landing page, though. One-pagers are composed of various sections, are richer in content, and can have a menu that takes visitors to different sections on the page instead of to different pages. This practical and increasingly popular solution is also perfect for browsing on mobile devices.

One of the reasons I use Strikingly is that their one-page websites work like a hybrid when you add a blog section. This opens blog posts as new pages and saves the day when it comes to SEO, for it lets you publish a lot more content and organize it in categories [39].

Pros:

- Simple, fast, modern, and trendy.
- Great for browsing on mobile devices.
- Has a potential for higher conversion rate.
- Much faster and easier to create and maintain.
- You can always upgrade to a multiple-page option.

Cons:

- Not great if you have a lot of content.
- Not great for complex websites.
- Can be bad for SEO (this, though, can be avoided).

Multi-page website

Creating a multi-page website will take more work since you'll have to design numerous pages instead of just one. It will also make the website harder to navigate on mobile devices, for it's much easier to scroll than press the buttons on the menu.

Unless you need multiple pages due to different activities or genres you'd like to present on separate pages, it might be best to avoid this option or slowly grow your website and switch to it later, when you have more content.

Pros:

- Good option if you need lots of different sections.
- Easier to organize various types of content.
- Can be better for SEO.

Cons:

- More complicated to build and maintain.
- Slower to load.
- Not great for browsing on mobile devices.

Content

The idea behind every website and the main reason why people visit them is to find information. People will most likely visit your website either because they would like to find out more about you or because you published a story or blog post they were interested in. Here is a list of topics visitors might expect to find on a website:

- Who are you? (Title, description, bio, about)
- What are you currently working on? (Books, blog…)
- What have you already published?
- Where can people buy your books?
- How can they contact you? (Contact form)
- Where else can they connect with you (Social media, book platforms, such as Goodreads…)?
- Can they subscribe to your newsletter and/or blog?
- Do you offer useful, relevant, and interesting content?

This information, starting with the title and description of your site, is also highly important for SEO and thus your website's ranking in browsers' search results. You'll find more on that in Chapter 11 *SEO & Google*.

UX and design

UX stands for user experience and it's one of the most important factors search engines consider when ranking your website. To create a good user experience, put yourself in the shoes of your visitors. Make it easy for them to find information, choose fonts that are easy to read, and colors and design that are not hard on the eyes.

Small fonts are hard to read and even more so on mobile devices. Using a light text on a dark background, as another example, might look stylish, but it will make reading longer text strenuous if not impossible.

The site should also load fast and be easy to navigate. Place the users and the site's functionality above everything else. Ideally, your site will look nice but never at the expense of user-experience, functionality, and speed. Good user-experience, though, is not related just to design.

Two of the most common technical issues that can ruin UX are slow loading time and dysfunctional links. Good website builders implement technical solutions to help you with SEO and load your site faster, and you can do a lot to improve or prevent these issues too.

Speed

A website will ideally load in a couple of seconds. The longer it takes for it to load and the slower it is to navigate, the worse UX this creates. This will have negative consequences, for speed is one of the main factors search engines consider when evaluating websites. While much depends on the hosting service, images are among the main culprits for slow websites. That's something you can easily improve.

Image size and compression

A website will take longer to load if you use too many images and/or too big and uncompressed images. Website builders usually publish the recommended image sizes and guidelines in their help sections. With open source and blogging platforms, though, this might depend more on the theme than the platform, so look for information on the developer's website.

Many website builders have a library of free images, and these are usually automatically compressed by the platform. If you are going to upload your own images, though, follow the guidelines. Strikingly, for instance, recommends that you keep the files of your images under 200 KB. Recommended file size is 50 KB [40].

File size, however, will also depend on the use of the image. If, for instance, you use it as a background image, it will need to be larger than a small profile pic or favicon. You will thus have to check for the recommend image size (in pixels) based on its placement on the website and then also make sure that it doesn't exceed the recommended file size (in bytes) [41].

You can use online design apps, such as Snappa or Canva to resize images and download them optimized for web. You can also use an open source program GIMP, but that's more complicated and takes a steeper learning curve.

11. SEO & GOOGLE

SEO stands for Search Engine Optimization. If you properly take care of it, it will bring more visitors to your website. That's why successful businesses put a lot of emphasis on SEO – it's a great way of getting organic traffic without spending a dime on promotion.

If you neglect it, though, and search engines detect any issues with your website, they will punish you by decreasing your website's rank or even stop showing your website in search results. After investing all the time and money into creating your website, you really don't want that to happen.

The good news is that this can be easily avoided. There are guidelines, apps, and tools that can help you check your website for any SEO issues and give you suggestions for improvements. Taking care of this should be a priority.

Website builders include SEO sections as a part of their dashboards and Strikingly even present the recommended steps in a form of a to-do list, so follow their suggestions. You'll need to purchase Business plan on WordPress.com to get access to the SEO features [42] and with WordPress.org, you'll have to buy a plugin for SEO.

To better understand how SEO works, take a look at some of the main factors search engines consider when evaluating a website:

- Security (SSL certificate)
- SEO tags on your website (title, description, meta tags)
- UX (fast, mobile friendly, easy to navigate, bounce rate…)
- Content and relevance
- Backlinks and referrals

SEO features on your website

SEO starts as soon as you start building your website. Things such as your website's title, description, favicon, and meta tags are all important parts of SEO.

Title and description

Title and your website's description are important for two reasons: first, they help search engines identify what your website is about and second, they'll appear in browsers' search results or in the posts shared on social media.

The title should include your name and role, such as a writer or author, since these serve as keywords. As for the description, it should further describe the purpose of your website. The recommended length of the description is about 150 characters – no more than a sentence or two.

If you specialize in a certain genre, you can make that clear in the title and description as well. You can also highlight your achievements. Put yourself in the shoes of someone who sees the link to your website in search results. If the website's title and description grab their attention, they might just click and visit your website [43].

Favicon

Favicon is a small icon you see at the top of tabs when you browse. It helps you see which website hides under which tab so that you can navigate between them easier. This is good for UX and looks professional.

You can prepare favicon as an image in PNG format. Favicons are displayed in a tiny size of 16x16 pixels, but you can usually upload a bit larger image and the platform will fix that for you. Just make sure it's a square.

Meta tags, blog, and page descriptions

It's highly recommended that you write a short description and create meta tags for every blog post, every page, and every image on your website. This is important because it helps search engines understand the content and suggest it to the users who might be interested in it.

You'll find meta tags and description options in your website builder's settings as well as blog post settings. For images, you should be able to see the meta tag option when you upload the image and before you insert it on the page.

UX evaluation

Search engines evaluate UX using various parameters, such as speed, performance on mobile devices, ease of use, bounce rate, and ads, to mention just a few. The main concern of Google and other search engines is to ensure that the visitors have a good experience [44].

If, for instance, it takes ages for the website to load or the users are bombarded with annoying pop-ups and ads, this will be reflected in a higher bounce rate and less time spent on the website – two clear indicators of a poor user experience.

This means that the users either didn't find what they were looking for, have experienced technical issues, or for some other reason didn't find the website enjoyable or useful.

Content and relevance

One of the most important factors for website's ranking is content. Websites that provide a lot of high-quality content rank higher. Having an interesting blog, for instance, is one of the best ways of getting more traffic from search engines.

Another important thing are keywords. If you are a writer, use related keywords, such as "writer," "author," or "books" in your website's title and description. Since people tried to game the system with a technique called "keyword stuffing," though, don't overdo it.

Google now above all looks for naturally flowing texts rather than keywords. Content, however, is not just text; it's everything else on your website, including images and ads – these too are a type of content. Everything should be relevant to the website's main purpose.

Backlinks and referrals

Another two important factors are backlinks and referrals. They stand for the traffic that is being sent to your website from the links published on other websites (backlinks) or external sources such as social media and emails (referrals).

Like your website, these sources too are evaluated by search engines. Not just any referral or backlink is of value, and some can do more harm than good. The more trustworthy and the higher ranking the source, the higher its worth.

Dysfunctional links

Broken, dysfunctional or dead links are a nuisance. This, however, happens easily, often, and to everyone. It's likely you too will have quite a few links on your website that, for some reason, won't lead to where they are supposed to.

The older your website, the more likely this is to happen. Regularly checking your website for broken links is thus advisable. Thankfully, you don't have to do this manually since there are online tools you can use.

I recommend *Online Broken Link Checker* [45] because it doesn't just show you the list of broken links but also helps you locate them. The tool will show you the exact location of the link in the HTML code of your website, which makes it easy to find it.

Google must-have SEO tools

Google have a lot of useful tools for marketing and SEO. The main ones you should start using are Google Webmasters, Google Search Console, and Google Analytics.

Google Webmasters

You'll find a lot of useful resources, guides, and other helpful content on Google Webmasters website [46]. That's the place where you can take free Webmaster Academy courses to learn the basics of SEO, find the design, quality, or technical guidelines, and test your website.

Google Search Console

Google Search Console is incredibly useful and important. You can register and verify the ownership of your website there, and if the Console then detects any issues, it will send you an email so that you'll know what to fix [47].

You'll also get insights into the search terms and keywords that brought visitors to your website as well as reports that can help you optimize and improve your website. Finally, you can connect Google Search Console to Google Analytics and get even more out of these two tools.

If you use Strikingly, you'll find easy-to-follow instructions on how to verify and register your site on Google in your website's settings and help section [48]. WordPress.com and other websites builders usually provide similar instructions.

Google Analytics

Google Analytics is a complex tool, but it's recommended that you use it too, for it provides information you otherwise won't be able to get. Like with Google Search Console, you'll have to add your website as a property and then verify it. Website builders and blog platforms make this quite easy.

You'll have to invest some time into learning how to use this tool, though. To make this easier, Google created Analytics Academy with free courses that will help you set everything up [49]. It's worth investing a bit of your time in this due to the benefits that far outweigh the initial trouble.

While you won't need everything Google Analytics' has to offer, some features are most useful even for small websites. You'll get valuable insight into things such as your website's bounce rate, traffic sources, demographics, browsers, and devices.

Bounce rate

Bounce rate is among the most important information about your website you can get. A bounce happens when a visitor doesn't interact with your website beyond the first page they visited. This includes not clicking on any link, button, or form.

While Google Analytics cannot tell you the reason for this, a high bounce rate means that there is something wrong with your website and you should fix it. Potential reasons for it could be technical issues (e.g. the site being too slow or not supported on certain browsers and devices), poor design and UX (e.g. hard to read, annoying ads or pop-ups), or content (not what the visitor expected or of poor quality).

In general, a good bounce rate stays below 50% and if you can get it below 30%, that's considered excellent [50]. It's highly unlikely, though, to see a bounce rate of zero since there are other reasons for bounces that have nothing to do with the website. The visitor, for instance, might be interrupted while browsing and Google Analytics counts inactivity as a bounce too.

Bounce rate also depends on content and the type of websites (e.g. blog, landing page...). Blogs, for instance, can have a higher bounce rate. If you write engaging content, use calls to actions (e.g. subscribe for my newsletter), and provide links to other interesting blog posts or resources, though, there's no reason for a high bounce rate.

Traffic sources and demographics

Another important piece of information is where the traffic to your website comes from. This will tell you how well you are doing on social media, which backlinks to your site bring the most traffic, and what kind of content leads to most visits. Based on that, you'll be able to decide what to focus on.

Demographics can tell you which countries your website get the most traffic from. Be careful with interpreting these results, though. Many advanced users nowadays use VPN services or incognito browsers such as Tor [51]. This allows them to hide or show a misleading location. Most people, however, don't do this, so you should still be able to get a broad idea of where your visitors are coming from.

Browsers and devices

Knowing what devices and browsers your visitors use is important for technical reasons. You need to make sure your website looks good across systems and devices, especially those your visitors prefer to use. Many website builders or themes might not work well on some browsers and Google Analytics will alert you to that.

You can view and filter the data for all types of devices (desktop, mobile, and tablet) as well as OS and browsers. If you, for instance, notice a high bounce rate on mobile devices but low on desktops, this suggests there's a technical issue with the mobile version. A good website builder or theme developer should prevent or fix this. If not, you'll have to switch to another platform or theme.

Other SEO apps and tools

Numerous apps and tools can help you check for any SEO issues and evaluate your website's health. While Google Search Console and Google Analytics offer useful insight, it doesn't hurt to use other apps and tools as well. They can give you additional information and valuable suggestions on how to improve your website's performance.

Just google "SEO checker" and you'll get a list of them. They are simple to use and it's easy to get your site analyzed. I suggest trying out more than one such app, though, since they are not 100% reliable and they do not all work in the same way. Some also give much better suggestions than others. You'll find the recommended ones in Chapter 12 *Useful Apps & Tools*.

12. USEFUL APPS & TOOLS

You already came across some of these apps in the previous chapters, but they are all listed here again so that you can easily find what you need when you need it. That's not all, though. Check the *Recommended reading* following this chapter too. You'll find more interesting information there.

For the latest news and updates, visit my website matejaklaric.com and subscribe for my monthly newsletter. Things change fast, so subscribing to my newsletter will keep you informed. Last, but not least, I'd really appreciate if you could post a review of this book in the online bookstore where you bought it or on platforms such as Goodreads or BookBub. Thank you and best of luck with your website!

Passwords

To better understand what makes a password secure and how long it would take for a hacker to crack it, use a password checker. Don't, however, use it to check any passwords you are actually using. The idea behind these tools is that you can test how hard it would be to crack a password given its length and the characters it's composed of.

Kaspersky Secure Password Check

Kaspersky Secure Password Check is fast, simple, and easy to use, a good option if you are short on time: https://password.kaspersky.com/.

Better Buy's Estimated Password Cracking Times

Better Buy's *Estimated Password Cracking Times* includes an in-depth explanation of how password security works and recommendations for best practices: https://www.betterbuys.com/estimating-password-cracking-times/.

Security

Online security is not something you could master once and for all. It keeps developing and changing in response to the new threats that are constantly evolving. To stay on top of it, start by taking a few courses and follow relevant blogs.

Cyber Security Education

Heimdal Security offers free security courses for beginners and small businesses. You can also subscribe for their blog: https://heimdalsecurity.com/security-education-resources.

Two-factor authentication

One of the best ways of protecting your social media accounts is the use of two-factor authentication. At the very least, set this up for your Google account – it will protect the Google's apps and tools you use, including Gmail.

You can visit *Two Factor Auth (2FA)* for a comprehensive list of apps, social, and email accounts that enable two-factor authentication: https://twofactorauth.org/

DNS propagation

After you connected your domain to your website, check the DNS code propagation status to see whether everything has been set up right. You can check that for A record or CNAME, depending on how you connected your domain (e.g. you'd check CNAME for Strikingly and A record for Tumblr). One of the tools you can use is *Global DNS Propagation Checker*: https://www.whatsmydns.net/

Images

The easiest way of resizing and compressing images is by using online design apps, such as Snappa or Canva. On Snappa, you can download images as web-optimized JPG. On Canva, use the JPG small file size image option. This, however, works well for photos but might not be as good for line art and favicons. In such cases, PNG file could be better:
Snappa: https://snappa.com/
Canva: https://www.canva.com/
GIMP: https://www.gimp.org/

Uptime checkers

Another thing you should monitor is the uptime of your website. It's impossible to do this manually since you cannot be online 24/7 and keep checking your website. Apps, however, make this very easy.

Uptime Robot

All you need to do is sign up and submit your website's URL to Uptime Robot. The app will send you an email whenever it detects that your website went down. In such case, contact your website hosting service or website builder and ask them to fix the problem:
https://uptimerobot.com.

Website and SEO checkers

It's also a good idea to regularly check your website's general health, SEO, and speed as well as broken links, and backlinks. Different apps were created for these purposes so here are a few suggestions.

Website Grader by HubSpot

Website Grader by HubSpot provides a basic evaluation of your website. The grade is calculated based on the website's performance, SEO, and security:
https://website.grader.com/.

Website Checker by Ionos

Ionos' 1&1 Website Checker is another app that checks the general state of your website and gives you useful suggestions for optimization:
https://www.ionos.com/tools/website-checker.

SEO Site Checkup

With SEO Site Checkup, you'll get a detailed insight into your website's SEO. One of the best things about this app is their Keywords Cloud Test. It shows you the most used keywords on your website in visual representation: https://seositecheckup.com/.

Sitechecker

Sitechecker is also a SEO evaluation tool that will generate a detail report on various parameters of your website. Among other things, you'll get Google User Experience Score: https://sitechecker.pro/.

GT Metrix

GT Metrix is specialized in analyzing your website's speed and gives you recommendations for improvement. It's also worth visiting their blog where they publish helpful guides: https://gtmetrix.com/.

Online Broken Link Checker

The main benefit of Online Broken Link Checker in is that it makes it easy to locate broken links by highlighting them in your website's HTML code: https://www.brokenlinkcheck.com/.

Backlink Checker by Ahref

It's important to know where your traffic is coming from. While Google Console and Google Analytics provide some insight into the backlinks to your website, you can get more useful information if you also use an app specialized in backlinks.

Backlink Checker by Ahref is a good choice since it has the most active crawlers in its app category and thus a huge database of links [52]. The app provides a detail report on your website's backlinks as well as their estimated value: https://ahrefs.com/backlink-checker.

Google Analytics Academy

While you can get a basic insight into your website's stats on your website's dashboard, this is of highly limited use. It's recommended that you also use Google Analytics. you can learn how to master it at free Google Analytics Academy: https://analytics.google.com/analytics/academy/.

RECOMMENDED READING

Top 20 Most Expensive Domain Names Ever Sold: 2016 List. Agrawal, H. (2018). [online] *Shout Me Loud*. [Accessed 5 Mar. 2019]. Available at: https://www.shoutmeloud.com/top-10-most-expensive-domain-names-ever-sold.html

How the Internet Travels Across Oceans. Satariano, A. (2019). [online] *The New York Times*. [Accessed 3 Feb. 2019] Available at: https://www.nytimes.com/interactive/2019/03/10/technology/internet-cables-oceans.html

What is SSL/TLS and do I need a secure email connection? [online] *Purple Dog*. [Accessed 10 Jan. 2019]. Available at: https://www.purpledogdesign.com/clients/knowledgebase/58/What-is-SSL-or-TLS-and-do-I-need-a-secure-email-connection.html

EPP Status Codes | What Do They Mean, and Why Should I Know? [online] *ICANN*. [Accessed 5 Apr. 2019]. Available at: https://www.icann.org/resources/pages/epp-status-codes-2014-06-16-en

What Is DNS Propagation and How Does It Work? [online] Wahab, G. (2016). *Square 2*. [Accessed 5 Mar. 2019]. Available at: https://www.square2marketing.com/blog/what-is-dns-propagation-and-how-does-it-work

Why a domain's root can't be a CNAME — and other tidbits
about the DNS. [online] *freeCodeCamp*. (2018).
[Accessed 13 Mar. 2019] Available at:
https://medium.freecodecamp.org/why-cant-a-domain-s-
root-be-a-cname-8cbab38e5f5c

Edward Snowden on Passwords. [online] *Last Week Tonight
with John Oliver (HBO)*. (2015). [Accessed 11 Apr.
2019]. Available at: https://youtu.be/yzGzB-yYKcc

WordPress Comprises 90% of Hacked Sites. [online]
Muncaster, P. (2019). *Infosecurity Magazine*. [Accessed
5 Jan. 2019]. Available at: https://www.infosecurity-
magazine.com/news/wordpress-comprises-90-of-
hacked-1-1/

Why do WordPress websites get hacked? [online]
Koukovistas, A. (2017). *Hallam*. [Accessed 5 Apr. 2019].
Available at: https://www.hallaminternet.com/wordpress-
website-hacked/

The Ultimate WordPress Security Guide – Step by Step
(2019). [online] *WPBeginner.com*. [Accessed 7 Apr.
2019]. Available at:
https://www.wpbeginner.com/wordpress-security/

What Is the True Cost of Building and Managing a
WordPress Website? [online] Morris, J. (2016).
Copyblogger. [Accessed 10 Apr. 2019]. Available at:
https://www.copyblogger.com/wordpress-website-cost/

How to Avoid Public Wi-Fi Security Risks. [online]
Kaspersky lab. [Accessed 5 Apr. 2019]. Available at:

https://www.kaspersky.com/resource-center/preemptive-safety/public-wifi-risks

VPN Beginner's Guide: What is a VPN and how does it work. [online] Mason, J. (2019). *TheBestVPN*. [Accessed 5 Apr. 2019]. Available at: https://thebestvpn.com/what-is-vpn-beginners-guide/

Future of Accelerated Mobile Pages (Google AMP) in 2019. [online] Yan, K. (2018). *Bravoka Digital Designs*. [Accessed 14 Apr. 2019]. Available at: https://bravoka.io/articles/accelerated-mobile-pages-2019/

Single-Page Websites: Are They Good or Bad for SEO?. [online] *Link-Assistant.Com* (2019). [Accessed 5 Apr. 2019]. Available at: https://www.link-assistant.com/news/one-page-website-seo.html

Search Engine Optimization (SEO) Starter Guide. [online] *Google Support*. [Accessed 5 Apr. 2019]. Available at: https://support.google.com/webmasters/answer/7451184

Find Out How You Stack Up to New Industry Benchmarks for Mobile Page Speed. [online] *Think with Google*. (2017). [Accessed 9 Apr. 2019]. Available at: https://www.thinkwithgoogle.com/marketing-resources/data-measurement/mobile-page-speed-new-industry-benchmarks/

Guidelines for a faster Shopify, Squarespace, Wix (or other website builders) website. [online] *GTmetrix*. (2018). [Accessed 5 Apr. 2019]. Available at:

https://gtmetrix.com/blog/guidelines-for-a-faster-shopify-squarespace-wix-or-other-website-builders-website/

Why You Shouldn't Trust Your Web Host's Uptime Guarantee. [online] Roach, J. (2018). *Cloudwards.* [Accessed 9 Apr. 2019]. Available at: https://www.cloudwards.net/uptime-guarantee/

REFERENCES

1

Internet 101. [online] *Khan Academy*. [Accessed 6 Apr. 2019]. Available at: https://www.khanacademy.org/computing/computer-science/internet-intro

2

International Targeting Report. [online] *Google Search Console Help*. [Accessed 6 Apr. 2019]. Available at: https://support.google.com/webmasters/answer/6059209

3

Why use www? [online] *www. is not deprecated*. [Accessed 11 Feb. 2019]. Available at: https://www.yes-www.org/why-use-www/

4

What's the difference between HTTP and HTTPS?. [online] Vukadinovic, D. (2018). *GlobalSign*. [Accessed 6 Apr. 2019]. Available at: https://www.globalsign.com/en/blog/the-difference-between-http-and-https/

5

The All-Time Top 20 All-Cash Domain Sales. (2003 to 2019) *DN Journal*. [online] [Accessed 6 Apr. 2019].

Available at:
http://www.dnjournal.com/archive/domainsales/dnjournal-all-time-top-20-cash-domain-sales.htm

6

Why do WordPress websites get hacked? [online]
Koukovistas, A. (2017). *Hallam*. [Accessed 5 Apr. 2019].
Available at: https://www.hallaminternet.com/wordpress-website-hacked/

7

What is SSL/TLS and do I need a secure email connection?
[online] *Purple Dog*. [Accessed 6 Apr. 2019]. Available
at:
https://www.purpledogdesign.com/clients/knowledgebase/58/What-is-SSL-or-TLS-and-do-I-need-a-secure-email-connection.html

8

How Every Cyber Attack Works. [online] Cucu, P. (2017).
Heimdal Security Blog. [Accessed 6 Apr. 2019].
Available at: https://heimdalsecurity.com/blog/cyber-attack/

9

The Ultimate Password Security Guide for Unhackable
Credentials. [online] Zaharia, A. (2016). *Heimdal
Security Blog*. [Accessed 6 Apr. 2019]. Available at:

https://heimdalsecurity.com/blog/password-security-guide/

10

About WHOIS. [online] *ICANN WHOIS*. (n.d.). [Accessed 6 Apr. 2019]. Available at: https://whois.icann.org/en/about-whois

11

EPP Status Codes | What Do They Mean, and Why Should I Know? [online] *ICANN WHOIS*. [Accessed 6 Apr. 2019]. Available at: https://www.icann.org/resources/pages/epp-status-codes-2014-06-16-en

12

3 Ways to Protect Your Email Address from Hackers and Spammers. [online] Kane, M. (2016). *Blogsite Studio*. [Accessed 6 Apr. 2019]. Available at: https://blogsitestudio.com/protect-email-address-hackers-spammers/

13

Registry Lock Service. [online] *Verisign*. [Accessed 6 Apr. 2019]. Available at: https://www.verisign.com/en_US/channel-resources/domain-registry-products/registry-lock/index.xhtml

14

WordPress Comprises 90% of Hacked Sites. [online] Muncaster, P. (2019). *Infosecurity Magazine.* [Accessed 5 Jan. 2019]. Available at: https://www.infosecurity-magazine.com/news/wordpress-comprises-90-of-hacked-1-1/

15

The Ultimate WordPress Security Guide – Step by Step (2019). [online] *WPBeginner.com.* [Accessed 7 Apr. 2019]. Available at: https://www.wpbeginner.com/wordpress-security/

16

5 Common WordPress Security Issues. [online] Wright, K. (2017). *iThemes.* [Accessed 7 Apr. 2019]. Available at: https://ithemes.com/wordpress-security-issues/

17

'All wifi networks' are vulnerable to hacking, security expert discovers. [online] Hern, A. (2017). *The Guardian.* [Accessed 7 Apr. 2019]. Available at: https://www.theguardian.com/technology/2017/oct/16/wpa2-wifi-security-vulnerable-hacking-us-government-warns

18

VPN Beginner's Guide: What is a VPN and how does it work. [online] Mason, J. (2019). *The Best VPN.* [Accessed 7 Apr. 2019]. Available at: https://thebestvpn.com/what-is-vpn-beginners-guide/

19

The Dangers of Shared Hosting. [online] Talalaev, A. (2018). *WebARX Security Blog.* [Accessed 7 Apr. 2019]. Available at: https://www.webarxsecurity.com/dangers-of-shared-hosting/

20

A Comparative Review of Shared Hosting vs Dedicated Hosting vs Cloud Hosting. [online] Khan, M. A. (2019). *The Official Cloudways Blog.* [Accessed 7 Apr. 2019]. Available at: https://www.cloudways.com/blog/wordpress-shared-vs-dedicated-vs-cloud-hosting/

21

cPanel & WHM Virtual Tour. [online] *cPanel.* [Accessed 7 Apr. 2019]. Available at: https://cpanel.net/products/trial/

22

cPanel Tutorials: Email Accounts. [video] *cPanelTV* (2015). [Accessed 9 Apr. 2019]. Available at:

https://www.youtube.com/watch?v=PwyO_burlT8&index
=3&list=PLZk46idJS6s7VPzwPQXNtwlsU23D3TqRV

23

Custom domains. [online] *Tumblr Help Center*. [Accessed 9
Apr. 2019]. Available at:
https://tumblr.zendesk.com/hc/en-us/articles/231256548-
Custom-domains

24

Connect Custom Domain. [online] Strikingly Help Center.
[Accessed 9 Apr. 2019]. Available at:
https://support.strikingly.com/hc/en-
us/articles/215046947-Connect-Custom-Domain

25

What Is DNS Propagation and How Does It Work? [online]
Wahhab, G. (2016). *Square2*. [Accessed 9 Apr. 2019].
Available at:
https://www.square2marketing.com/blog/what-is-dns-
propagation-and-how-does-it-work

26

Global DNS Propagation Checker. [online] Wall, D. *What's
My DNS?* [Accessed 9 Apr. 2019]. Available at:
https://www.whatsmydns.net/

27

What is a 301 Redirect? [online] Gotch, N. *Gotch SEO*.
[Accessed 9 Apr. 2019]. Available at:
https://www.gotchseo.com/301-redirects/

28

Find Out How You Stack Up to New Industry Benchmarks
for Mobile Page Speed. [online] *Think with Google*.
(2017). [Accessed 9 Apr. 2019]. Available at:
https://www.thinkwithgoogle.com/marketing-
resources/data-measurement/mobile-page-speed-new-
industry-benchmarks/

29

Why You Shouldn't Trust Your Web Host's Uptime
Guarantee. [online] Roach, J. (2018). *Cloudwards*.
[Accessed 9 Apr. 2019]. Available at:
https://www.cloudwards.net/uptime-guarantee/

30

Updates to mobile page speed score on the Landing Pages
tab. [online] *Google Ads Help*. (2019). [Accessed 9 Apr.
2019]. Available at: https://support.google.com/google-
ads/answer/9238823

31

Incompatible Plugins. [online] *WordPress.com Support*.
[Accessed 9 Apr. 2019]. Available at:
https://en.support.wordpress.com/incompatible-plugins/

32

Best WordPress Managed Hosting 2019. [online] Stevens,
J. (2019). *Hosting Facts*. [Accessed 9 Apr. 2019].
Available at: https://hostingfacts.com/wordpress-
managed-hosting-review/

33

Why do WordPress websites get hacked? [online]
Koukovistas, A. (2017). *Hallam*. [Accessed 5 Apr. 2019].
Available at: https://www.hallaminternet.com/wordpress-
website-hacked/

34

Why won't the Tumblr staff reply to my ticket? [online] Kretts,
T. (2018). *Quora*. [Accessed 10 Apr. 2019]. Available at:
https://www.quora.com/Why-wont-the-Tumblr-staff-reply-
to-my-ticket

35

Portfolio themes for WordPress and Tumblr. [online]
Precrafted. [Accessed 10 Apr. 2019]. Available at:
https://precrafted.com/ https://precrafted.com/

36

How to Use, Install & Change Tumblr Themes. [online]
    Theme Junkie. [Accessed 10 Apr. 2019]. Available at:
    https://www.theme-junkie.com/how-to-use-install-
    change-tumblr-themes/

37

The Story of the Fox and White Rabbit landing page. [online]
    Klaric, M. [Accessed 10 Apr. 2019]. Available at:
    https://www.the-fox-and-white-rabbit.com

38

What Is the True Cost of Building and Managing a
    WordPress Website? [online] Morris, J. (2016).
    Copyblogger. [Accessed 10 Apr. 2019]. Available at:
    https://www.copyblogger.com/wordpress-website-cost/

39

Single-Page Websites: Are They Good or Bad for SEO?
    [online] Stepanova, K. (2017). *Link-Assistant.Com*.
    [Accessed 10 Apr. 2019]. Available at: https://www.link-
    assistant.com/news/one-page-website-seo.html

40

Increase Search Engine Ranking (SEO). [online] *Strikingly
    Help Center*. (2018). [Accessed 10 Apr. 2019]. Available
    at: https://support.strikingly.com/hc/en-
    us/articles/214364918

41

Background Sizes & Settings - Guidelines for background images. [online] *Strikingly Help Center*. (2019). [Accessed 10 Apr. 2019]. Available at: https://support.strikingly.com/hc/en-us/articles/214364898-Check-Background-Sizes-Settings

42

Two Factor Auth List. [online] Davis, J. [Accessed 10 Apr. 2019]. Available at: https://twofactorauth.org/

43

How to Write Meta Descriptions that Drive Clicks and Conversions. [online] *Shopify*. (2018) [Accessed 10 Apr. 2019]. Available at: https://www.shopify.com/blog/how-to-write-meta-descriptions

44

How UX fits into SEO. [online] Chambers, J. (2018). *Search Engine Watch*. [Accessed 10 Apr. 2019]. Available at: https://searchenginewatch.com/2018/06/28/how-ux-fits-into-seo/

45

Online Broken Link Checker. [online] *Brokenlinkcheck.com*. [Accessed 10 Apr. 2019]. Available at: https://www.brokenlinkcheck.com/.

46

Google Webmasters. [online] *Google*. [Accessed 10 Apr. 2019]. Available at: https://www.google.com/webmasters/learn/

47

Google Search Console. [online] *Google*. [Accessed 10 Apr. 2019]. Available at: https://search.google.com/search-console/about

48

Google Search Console (Webmaster Tools) / Google Sitemap. [online] *Strikingly Help Center*. (2019). [Accessed 10 Apr. 2019]. Available at: https://support.strikingly.com/hc/en-us/articles/214364728

49

Google Analytics Academy. [online] *Google*. [Accessed 10 Apr. 2019]. Available at: https://analytics.google.com/analytics/academy/

50

What is Considered a Good Bounce Rate for a Blog? [online] Parsons, J. *Blogpros*. [Accessed 10 Apr. 2019]. Available at: https://blogpros.com/blog/2016/09/what-good-bounce-rate

51

The Tor Project | Privacy & Freedom Online. [online] *Tor Project*. [Accessed 10 Apr. 2019]. Available at: https://www.torproject.org/about/history/

52

A Closer Look at the Most Active Good Bots. [online] Zeifman, I. and Breslaw, D. (2017). *Imperva*. [Accessed 11 Apr. 2019]. Available at: https://www.imperva.com/blog/most-active-good-bots/

About the author

Mateja started to write short stories at the age of ten and later became a freelance journalist, radio personality, and explorer of the inner worlds. To make life even more fun, she also ran an advertising agency for eight years. Apart from that, Mateja's life resembles a roller coaster ride full of ups and downs and some pretty wild turns. Among other things, her car was destroyed by tanks, and she survived several brushes with death. Mateja graduated in psychology from Arizona State University and is now a writer, photographer, and transformational guide.

matejaklaric.com

Also by Mateja Klaric

Self-Publishing Made Easy, Book 1
How to Self-Publish Your Book:
The Fast, Free & Easy Way

A step-by-step guide to the technical aspects of self-publishing for absolute beginners. It will teach you how to format your book in MS Word, prepare and format images for print, design your book cover using free tools, and more. You will get a general overview of everything you need to self-publish your first book the fast, free, and easy way.

Self-Publishing Made Easy, Book 2
You Self-Published, Now What?
How to Promote Your Book

A guide to cost-efficient book promotion for writers on a budget that can be used as a blueprint for recommended activities. It includes real-life examples, step-by-step instructions, evaluation of costs and revenue, the list of best apps and tools, useful tips, and more. This is book two in the 'Self-Publishing Made Easy' series. For instructions on how to self-publish a book, refer to book one by the same author.

The Fox & White Rabbit, Book 1

The Story of the Fox and White Rabbit

(not your ordinary fable)

The fox leads a cruel and merciless life until one night in the woods changes everything. A chance meeting with magical White Rabbit leaves the fox shaken to the core. Nothing will ever be the same again.

Made in the USA
Middletown, DE
27 June 2019